What Kind of Animal Is It?

Birds of All Kinds

Rebecca Sjonger & Bobbie Kalman

A Crabtree Crown Book

Crabtree Publishing

crabtreebooks.com

Birds of All Kinds

Editor-in-chief
Bobbie Kalman

Writing team
Rebecca Sjonger
Bobbie Kalman

Substantive editor
Kelley MacAulay

Editors
Molly Aloian
Robin Johnson
Reagan Miller
Kathryn Smithyman

Design
Samara Parent

Consultant
Patricia Loesche, Ph.D., Animal Behavior Program, Department of Psychology, University of Washington

Production manager
Candice Campbell

Photographs
Shutterstock

Illustrations
Katherine Kantor : page 31

Crabtree Publishing

crabtreebooks.com 800-387-7650

In Canada: We acknowledge the financial support of the Government of Canada through the Canada Book Fund for our publishing activities.

Printed in the U.S.A./CP032026

Published in Canada
Crabtree Publishing
616 Welland Ave.
St. Catharines,
Ontario L2M 5V6

Published in the United States
Crabtree Publishing
347 Fifth Ave.
Suite 1402-145
New York, NY 10016

Hardcover: 978-1-0398-7315-5
Paperback: 978-1-0398-7373-5
Ebook (pdf): 978-1-0398-7422-0
Epub: 978-1-0398-7471-8

Library and Archives Canada Cataloguing in Publication
Available at Library and Archives Canada

Library of Congress Cataloging-in-Publication Data
Available at the Library of Congress

Contents

Birds of all kinds

A bird is an animal that has a beak and feathers. There are many kinds of birds. Birds live all over the world. How many kinds of birds do you know?

red-winged blackbird

Some birds **perch** in trees. To perch means to sit. Cardinals and red-winged blackbirds perch in trees.

cardinal

Some birds stay close to the ground. They almost never fly! Red grouses stay close to the ground.

red grouse

bald eagle

Some birds hunt and eat other animals. Bald eagles hunt and eat other animals.

emperor penguin

Canada goose

Some birds live near water. Geese live near water.

Some birds cannot fly. Penguins and ostriches cannot fly.

ostrich

Bird bodies

Birds have two wings and two legs. They are **warm-blooded** animals. The bodies of warm-blooded animals stay warm, even in cold places.

Breathing air

All birds must breathe air to stay alive. Birds breathe air using **lungs**. Lungs are body parts that take in air. They also let out air. All birds have two lungs.

Feathers help a bird fly. Feathers also keep a bird's body warm and dry.

A bird has two feet. It uses its feet to walk. A bird may also use its feet to carry food.

Backbones

All birds have **backbones**. A backbone is a group of bones in the middle of an animal's back.

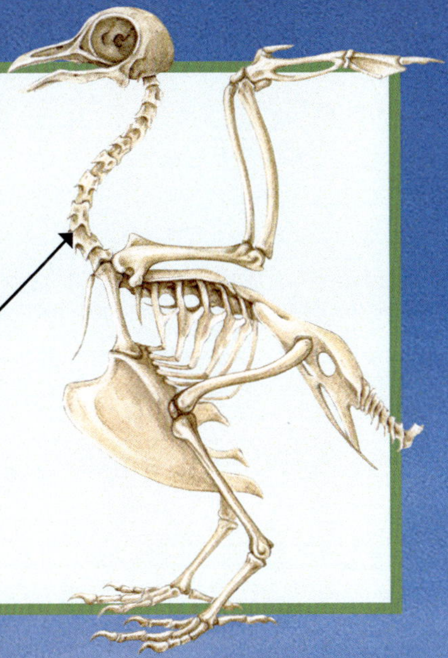

Feathers

Birds are covered with feathers. They have soft fluffy feathers near their skin. These fluffy feathers are called **down**. Down keeps birds warm.

Flying feathers

Birds also have strong, stiff feathers. These feathers cover the soft feathers. Stiff feathers help birds fly.

Birds that fly have strong, stiff feathers on their wings.

This baby hawk is covered in down. When it gets older, its flying feathers will grow on top of its down. The bird will then look like the adult hawk beside it.

So many colors!

Different birds have feathers of different colors. Some birds have feathers that help the birds hide. The colors of the feathers match the places where the birds live. Other birds have bright, colorful feathers. Male peacocks have colorful feathers. The bird below is a male peacock.

Some owls hide in trees when they hunt or sleep. The colors of their feathers help the owls hide.

Made for flying

Most birds can fly. Birds use their wings to take off and land. In the air, birds **flap** their wings to move and turn. Birds flap their wings by moving them up and down.

Birds must flap their wings many times to take off.

A light body

A bird has **hollow bones**. Hollow bones have empty spaces inside them. Hollow bones make a bird's body light. Having a light body helps a bird fly.

A bird's bone

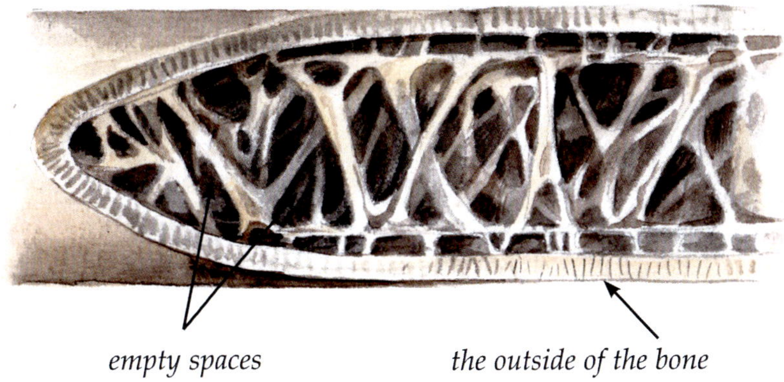

Why birds fly

Flying helps birds stay alive. When birds cannot find food in one place, they can fly to another place to find food. Birds also fly when other animals are hunting them. The birds below are flying away from a jackal that is looking for dinner!

What do birds eat?

Different birds eat different foods. Some birds eat plant foods such as seeds. Animals that eat plant foods are called **herbivores**. Some birds eat animals. Animals that eat other animals are called **carnivores**.

Sunbirds are herbivores. They eat **nectar**. *Nectar is a sweet liquid found in flowers.*

Puffins are carnivores. They eat fish. How many fish did the puffin find for food?

Finding food

Birds do not like to share their meals with other birds! Most birds look for food alone, but some birds look for food in groups. Looking for food in groups can help birds find more to eat.

The birds in this picture are common terns. Common terns sometimes look for food in groups.

Feeding babies

Some young birds need their parents to feed them. The parents fly away to find food. They bring back the food to their babies. The young birds open their mouths when their parents return with the food. The parents drop small pieces of food into the mouths of the babies.

Birds all over

Birds live almost everywhere on Earth. They make homes in dry places, in wet places, in warm places, and in cold places. The natural places where animals live are called **habitats**. Some bird habitats are forests, fields, deserts, and places that are near water. Some birds even live in the coldest parts of the world, such as Antarctica!

Birds that live in warm places often have brightly colored feathers.

Penguins live in the freezing waters of Antarctica.

Canada geese live near water. They fly to warm places before the water freezes.

Time to fly!

Some birds live in places where the winters are cold. When the cold weather comes in autumn, most of these birds fly to warm places. The warm places are far away. The birds stay in the warm places for winter. They fly back home in spring.

Nest sweet nest!

Most birds make **nests**. Nests are warm, safe places where birds lay their eggs. When the babies hatch from the eggs, they live in the nests. Some nests are hidden in leafy trees and plants. Other are hidden on the ground. Birds hide their nests so other animals will not eat their eggs or babies.

This bird has some grass in its beak for making a nest.

This nest is on the ground. The grasses and dirt around the nest help hide it.

Nest builders

Nests can be many shapes and sizes. Different kinds of birds make nests using different things. Birds may use leaves, twigs, feathers, and mud to build their nests.

This weaver used straw to build its nest. The nest looks like a basket.

This egret parent has made a nest from branches and leaves.

Eggs and chicks

Not all bird eggs are the same size or color, but most eggs are oval-shaped. The oval shape makes eggs strong. Eggs must be strong because parent birds sit on the eggs. Sitting on the eggs keeps the **chicks** inside warm. Chicks are baby birds.

robin's egg

tern's egg

pheasant's egg

osprey's egg

cassowary's egg

A booby warms its eggs with its feet.

Young birds

After the chicks hatch, they stay in their nests. Some chicks stay in the nests for a few weeks. Others stay for a few months. Parent birds keep their chicks warm and safe in the nests. Most parents stay with their chicks until the young birds are ready to live on their own.

This baby hawk will stay in the nest until it learns to fly.

In the trees

Birds that perch in trees have long toes. Their toes can curl around the tree branches. Birds that perch build their nests in trees. They find food close to where they live.

Many birds that perch have small bodies.

This bird is called a pied wagtail. It eats insects that live in trees.

Many birds that perch in trees are songbirds. Songbirds can sing! Songbirds sing to find other birds. They also sing to keep some birds away. This mockingbird is a songbird.

wild turkeys

On the ground

chickens

Some birds live on the ground and hardly ever fly. The wings of these birds are weak, but their legs and feet are strong for walking. Turkeys and chickens are birds that live on the ground. They can fly, but they cannot fly far.

Life on land

Some birds that live on the ground build nests near the ground. They also look for food close to the ground. Most of these birds eat plants and insects. This bird is a francolin. It eats berries, plants, and insects.

In the water

Some birds live near rivers, ponds, lakes, and oceans. Many birds that live near water are good swimmers. Birds that swim have **webbed feet**. Webbed feet have skin between the toes. Birds use their webbed feet to paddle in the water. Many birds that swim dive down to find fish and other foods.

Trumpeter swans eat only plants.
As they swim, they put their heads down into the water to bite off plants to eat.

Close to land

Some birds make their nests along the water's edge. They find their food in shallow water. These birds have long legs so they can walk in water. Their toes spread wide apart to help them stand in sand and mud. Birds that live along the water's edge have long thin beaks.

Birds that live near the water's edge catch tiny worms and shrimps in their beaks.

Birds that hunt

The bodies of some birds are built for hunting animals. Birds that hunt are good fliers. They have sharp, curved claws called **talons**. They use their talons to catch and carry food. Birds that hunt use their sharp beaks to tear food into pieces so they can eat it.

Bald eagles catch fish and other animals to eat. This bald eagle is about to catch a fish.

Hunting

Some birds hunt during the day. Daytime hunters see very well. They can see the animals they are hunting from high in the sky. Other birds hunt at night. Most nighttime hunters have good hearing. Owls can hear small animals that are moving around in the dark.

Secretary birds catch snakes and other animals to eat. They stomp on the animals using their strong legs and big feet.

Birds that cannot fly

A few kinds of birds cannot fly. Birds that cannot fly have big bodies and small wings. Their small wings cannot lift their big bodies into the air. Birds that cannot fly must walk or swim. They have strong legs and feet to carry them.

Penguins flap their wings under water to help them swim.

Cassowaries do not need to fly away from danger. They attack their enemies with their sharp claws.

Rheas have large wings, but they cannot fly. Sometimes they flap their wings as they run. They flap their wings to change direction!

Kiwis have wings, but their wings are very small. You can hardly see them!

An ostrich has very strong feet. It can run faster than any other bird can.

Create your own birds

Some birds look different than the birds you usually see. Their feathers may be long or spiky. The feathers of other birds may be very colorful. Most colorful birds live in places with hot weather.

black-crowned crane

quetzal

lilac-breasted roller

Choose different parts

You can create your own bird by putting the bodies of two or three kinds of birds together. Flip through this book and look at some birds.

How will your bird look?

Will your bird be colorful or plain? Will the bird have a long or short tail? Think about what your bird will eat. What kind of beak will it need? Will it have a long, thin beak or a short, curved beak? Will it have long or short leg? Will your bird have a crown of feathers on its head?

Draw it and color it

When you have decided on how your bird will look, draw a picture of it. Color your picture with crayons or paint. Have your friends make up birds, too. Display your bird art in your classroom, the library, or in the hallway of your school.

Words to know and Index

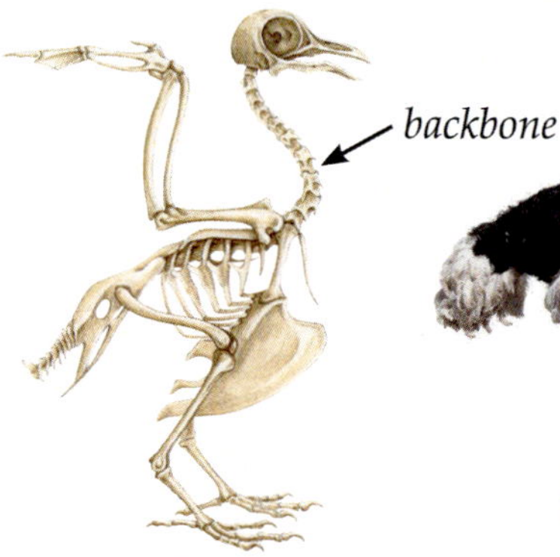